Original title:
Clouds of Slumber

Copyright © 2024 Creative Arts Management OÜ
All rights reserved.

Author: Wyatt Kensington
ISBN HARDBACK: 978-9916-90-592-0
ISBN PAPERBACK: 978-9916-90-593-7

Sanctuary in the Softening Light

In the dusk, the whispers glow,
The trees sway soft, a gentle show.
Shadows dance, the day's retreat,
In this space, the heart finds beat.

Golden rays through branches weave,
Nature's touch makes weary grieve.
A tranquil air, a soothing balm,
In the quiet, the spirit's calm.

Across the fields, where soft winds blow,
Fading light, a warm tableau.
Dreams unfold as stars ignite,
This sanctuary feels just right.

Moments linger, time stands still,
In the soft glow, each heart can fill.
With peace embraced and worries light,
We find our way in the softening light.

Echoes of a Gentle Slumber

In twilight's arms, where dreams commence,
A lullaby in silence dense.
The moonlight drapes a tender sheet,
Cradling all in soft retreat.

Whispers of the night unwind,
Pillow thoughts, so sweetly kind.
Hushed tones weave through the air,
A symphony beyond compare.

Stars punctuate the velvet sky,
In slumber's grasp, the world goes by.
Life's burdens fade, the mind takes flight,
In this haven, all feels right.

As shadows blend and softly sway,
Echoes of dreams guide the way.
In gentle slumber, hearts align,
Awake refreshed when morning shines.

Unraveling the Nighttime Dreams

Softly whispers call the mind,
In shadows deep, our thoughts unwind.
Stars above begin to gleam,
Nestled tight, we drift and dream.

Mysteries in moonlit beams,
Twisted fates and tangled themes.
Fingers trace the velvet air,
Hopes and wishes everywhere.

Echoes of a world unseen,
Stories spin in silver sheen.
Wander where the wild hearts roam,
In the depths, we find our home.

As dawn approaches, dreams do fade,
But in our hearts, the night's parade.
Hold the magic in your soul,
For nighttime dreams can make us whole.

Whispers of the Dreamscape

In twilight's hush, the stories bloom,
Awakening in shadowed room.
Silken threads of thought entwine,
Painting pictures, pure divine.

Winds of change begin to sigh,
As stars twinkle in the sky.
Mirrored pools of memory,
Show the path we long to see.

Floating through the cosmic sea,
Dancing notes of harmony.
Lightly tread on whispered air,
Finding solace everywhere.

Embrace the dreams that softly call,
In every rise and every fall.
For in each moment, we create,
A tapestry of love and fate.

Beneath the Feathered Veil

Velvet night with stars aligned,
Secrets woven, gently bind.
Whispers weave a soft cocoon,
Guarding dreams beneath the moon.

Feathers drift on silent breeze,
Brushing past like whispered pleas.
In the dark, the magic grows,
Through the stillness, the heart knows.

Time stands still; the shadows sway,
Leading minds where spirits play.
Underneath the sky so wide,
We shall journey, side by side.

With every breath, the visions flow,
In the night, our spirits glow.
Cherish tales that night unveils,
As we wander beneath the veils.

Embracing the Midnight Mist

In the embrace of midnight mist,
Whispers of the night persist.
Shadows dance with gentle grace,
Every dream finds its own place.

Fog enwraps the world in dreams,
Softly glimmers, silver beams.
Lost in thought, we breathe it in,
As the magic starts to spin.

Footsteps echo on the ground,
Secrets in the stillness found.
Gentle sighs from night's own heart,
In this realm, we play our part.

Awake the dreams that softly call,
Hold them close; don't let them fall.
For in this mist, we find a light,
Embracing all the stars so bright.

Sighs of the Celestial Canopy

Under the stars, whispers float,
Dreams meander, softly note.
A twinkle here, a shimmer bright,
A dance of shadows in the night.

Veils of darkness, secrets shared,
Softly cradled, hearts laid bare.
Moonlight baths the world anew,
In the silence, love shines through.

Drowsy Reveries

Gentle winds in twilight sigh,
Lingering thoughts as time slips by.
Slumbering songbirds find their rest,
In sleepy tunes, the heart feels blessed.

Clouds drift slowly, dreams descend,
Whispers of night, never end.
Lost in moments, soft and sweet,
In drowsy dreams, our souls do meet.

A Serenade for the Nocturnal

The owls hoot their lonely tune,
Underneath the silver moon.
Crickets play their midnight song,
In the night where we belong.

Stars align, a cosmic dance,
Inviting hearts to take a chance.
With every note, the shadows sway,
As night transforms into day.

The Slumbering Canvas Above

Canvas wide, the heavens stretch,
Painted hues in twilight etched.
Softest blues and velvet black,
In each moment, beauty lacks.

Dreamers gaze at wonders high,
The canvas whispers, clouds drift by.
In stillness wrapped, the night does weave,
A tapestry of night, believe.

Beneath the Softened Canopy

Beneath the leaves where shadows play,
The whispering winds come out to sway.
Nature's song in quiet light,
A haven found in soft twilight.

Moonlight dances on the ground,
As sleepy creatures stir around.
Crickets sing a lullaby,
Beneath a vast, enchanting sky.

Flowers close, their petals tight,
Dreams take flight in gentle night.
Stars above begin to gleam,
In this world, we dare to dream.

Here within this sacred dome,
The heart finds peace, the spirit home.
Beneath the canopy we share,
Our whispers float, a breath of air.

The Rhythm of Night's Embrace

In the quiet, shadows creep,
As the world falls into sleep.
Stars awaken, softly bright,
Setting rhythm to the night.

The moon's glow wraps all in grace,
A silver touch upon each face.
Whispers linger, secrets spun,
In the dance of dusk begun.

Rustling leaves and distant calls,
Echo in the night's vast halls.
Every heartbeat finds its place,
In the rhythm of night's embrace.

Time stands still, the hour late,
Wrapped in dreams, we contemplate.
In this symphony so fine,
The night invites our souls to shine.

Echoes in the Dreaming Realm

In twilight's hush, the echoes call,
Through corridors of dreams, we fall.
Visions dance in shadows cast,
Fleeting moments, fading fast.

Whispers linger on the breeze,
Carrying tales of ancient trees.
Floating softly, hopes arise,
Captured in the starlit skies.

Time unravels, threads entwine,
In this realm, our hearts align.
Every thought a gentle stream,
Flowing through the secret dream.

As night embraces all we know,
In silken clouds, our spirits flow.
In the echoes, we will find,
A universe within the mind.

Lullabies in the Ether

In the night, soft voices sing,
Lullabies that comfort bring.
Floating softly on the air,
Whispers of a world so rare.

Stars above in gentle twine,
Each a note, a sacred sign.
Moonbeams weave their silver thread,
As we drift to dreams, unfed.

In the ether, secrets blend,
Mending hearts that need to mend.
Every sigh is sweet and deep,
In this lullaby of sleep.

Let the night embrace us tight,
Cradling souls till morning light.
In the hush of starlit skies,
Lullabies continue to rise.

Twilight's Cradle

In the hush of dusk's embrace,
Stars awaken, take their place.
Shadows dance on fading light,
Whispers weave the coming night.

Crickets sing their evening song,
Nature hums, the dusk is long.
Moonbeams paint the world anew,
Softly cloaked in silver hue.

Embracing the Gossamer Nights

Silken threads in moonlit air,
Dreams unfold without a care.
Voices echo, soft and low,
In the night where wishes flow.

Stars like secrets twinkle bright,
Guarding hopes within the night.
Embrace the warmth of twilight's kiss,
Lost in moments filled with bliss.

Dreams Woven in Twilight

Threads of night and day entwined,
In the quiet, dreams aligned.
Horizon glows with painted skies,
As softly whispered dreams arise.

Every shadow holds a tale,
In the breeze, whispers sail.
Heartbeats echo, soft and true,
In the twilight, dreams renew.

The Weight of Skyward Hush

Veils of night descend like grace,
Wrapped in stillness, time slows pace.
Stars that shimmer, distant, bright,
Fill the canvas of the night.

Each breath taken, soft and deep,
Carried in the hush we keep.
In this moment, still and vast,
The weight of silence holds us fast.

Swaying in Moonlight's Cradle

In soft embrace, the shadows play,
Whispers of night, drifting away.
Stars above, a shimmering dance,
Crickets sing, in night's romance.

Underneath the silver glow,
Gentle breezes start to flow.
Dreams arise on twilight's beam,
Lost in the moon's tender dream.

The Peace of Shrouded Whispers

Silent winds weave tales untold,
In hallowed night, secrets unfold.
Leaves murmur soft, in hush profound,
In the calm, solace is found.

Moonbeams cast a gentle sway,
Fading worries drift away.
Every breath a quiet song,
In this peace, we all belong.

Night's Gentle Tapestry

Stars stitched in a velvet sky,
Woven dreams that float and fly.
Crimson clouds drift softly near,
Painting night with every tear.

The world beneath, in silence sleeps,
While the moon its watch still keeps.
A tapestry of tranquil sights,
Embraced within the arms of nights.

The Elysian Haze of Rest

In twilight's fog, so soft and bright,
Comfort whispers through the night.
Closed eyes find a sweet retreat,
Where life's burdens meet defeat.

Elysium calls on wings of dreams,
Serenity flows in gentle streams.
In the stillness, love's embrace,
Time stands still in this sacred place.

The Fabric of Serene Nights

In the hush of evening's grace,
Stars weave dreams in a silent place.
Moonlight dances on silver streams,
Whispers of peace wrap our sweet dreams.

A tapestry of soft, dark blue,
Embracing the world, quiet and true.
Each glimmer a wish, a thought set free,
In the fabric of nights that cradle thee.

Gentle winds carry secret sighs,
As night unfolds beneath the skies.
Time pauses in this sacred hour,
Nature's breath is a floating flower.

As dawn hints at the night's retreat,
We hold the magic in every beat.
Serene nights fade, yet still remain,
In the heart's memory, soft like rain.

A Caress of Gossamer Hues

In twilight's fold, colors unfurl,
Gossamer threads in a dancing swirl.
Soft pastels kiss the fading light,
A soothing warmth in the coming night.

Petals drift on a tender breeze,
Whispers of love within the trees.
Crimson and gold brush against the sky,
As evening descends with a gentle sigh.

Each hue a story, softly told,
In the canvas of night, brave and bold.
Starlight glimmers, a painter's hand,
In the twilight glow, we make our stand.

With every heartbeat, colors blend,
Creating a silence where dreams ascend.
A caress from the heavens above,
In gossamer hues, we find our love.

Celestial Drift of the Night

As shadows stretch and daylight fades,
Celestial drift in the cosmic glades.
Stars begin their luminous flight,
Guiding our thoughts through the velvet night.

Constellations whisper tales of old,
In symbols of silver, ancient and bold.
A tapestry woven in endless space,
Inviting us into a wondrous embrace.

Planets drift in their silent dance,
Each orbit a spell, a timeless trance.
The galaxy hums in a soothing tune,
Beneath the watchful gaze of the moon.

In the stillness, our spirits soar,
Through cosmic realms, forevermore.
Celestial wonders fill our sight,
As we drift in the arms of the night.

A Kiss from the Ethereal

In the twilight's glow, a whisper near,
An ethereal kiss, delicate and clear.
Soft as a feather, light as a wish,
Wrapped in the warmth of a moonlit swish.

Fragrant dreams float on silken air,
Carried on breezes, devoid of care.
The night serenades with a gentle refrain,
Each note a promise, a sweet, soft gain.

Enchanted moments, fleeting yet bright,
Canvas of darkness painted with light.
Each star, a sparkle of hope anew,
In the kiss of the night, it feels so true.

As dreams dissolve in the dawn's embrace,
We hold the magic of that sacred space.
A kiss from the heavens, so soft and wise,
Forever imprinted in our hearts' skies.

The Stillness of Nightfall's Gaze

The sky fades into a deep blue,
Stars awaken in their silent cue.
Moonlight dances on the shimmering lake,
In the stillness, the world seems to wake.

Whispers of wind brush past the trees,
Carrying secrets with gentle ease.
In shadows cast by the twilight's grace,
Time pauses for a delicate embrace.

A Gem of Rest in Time's Fabric

Nestled softly in the arms of night,
A treasure of peace, a hopeful sight.
Every moment, a delicate weave,
In the tapestry where dreams believe.

Gentle whispers cradle the hour,
In silent corners, memories flower.
Wrapped in solace, like a love's tune,
Time's fabric glimmers beneath the moon.

Echoes of Nature's Serenity

Leaves rustle softly in the cool breeze,
Nature's orchestra plays with such ease.
Birds chirp sweetly a lullaby song,
In the heart of the wild, where we belong.

Mountains stand guard, proud and tall,
Guardians of peace, answering the call.
In every whisper, in every sigh,
Nature's echoes softly harmonize.

The Crystal Veins of Slumber

In the hush of dusk, dreams start to flow,
Crystal veins of slumber gently glow.
With each heartbeat, the night unfolds,
Secrets of the soul in whispers told.

Rest now, dear heart, in this tender space,
Let lullabies dance in a warm embrace.
In stillness found beneath the stars,
The world once more heals from its scars.

Mellow Mists of Repose

In the morning's gentle sigh,
Mellow mists begin to rise.
Whispers of the dawn draw near,
Softly wrapping dreams in cheer.

Fields awake beneath the light,
Golden rays dispel the night.
Nature hums a soothing tune,
While the sky bursts into bloom.

The Soft Glow of Twilight Reverie

As daylight fades to dusky hue,
The soft glow invites the blue.
Stars peep through the velvet veil,
In twilight's calm, dreams set sail.

Crickets sing their evening song,
A serenade that feels so strong.
Memories dance in fading light,
Eager hearts take flight tonight.

Celestial Pillows of Night

Underneath the starry dome,
Celestial pillows call us home.
Wrapped in darkness, peace unfurls,
Dreams take shape in quiet swirls.

Moonlight bathes the world in grace,
We find solace in this space.
Gently drifting, hearts will soar,
While the night whispers, 'Explore.'

A Symphony of Sleep's Caress

Night descends with tender care,
A symphony fills the air.
Softly cradled, time stands still,
In this magic, hearts will thrill.

With every note, the spirits fly,
Sweet release as dreams pass by.
In the hush, we find a way,
To chase our worries far away.

Echoes of the Silent Abyss

In shadows deep, where whispers dwell,
Echoes call from the depths of hell.
A void that clings to breath and thought,
In silence lost, a battle fought.

Waves of darkness roll and sweep,
Through hollow halls, the secrets creep.
A haunting tune, an endless sigh,
In the abyss, where dreams go dry.

Hope flickers like a candle's flame,
In the abyss, it can't be tamed.
Yet, through the depths, a voice will rise,
A beacon bright in starry skies.

From the silent void, we find our truth,
In echoes dim, we seek our youth.
A journey's end, a brand new start,
In every echo, we heal the heart.

In the Arms of Starlit Dreams

Beneath the vast and glowing night,
Stars will whisper, soft and bright.
In their embrace, we drift and sway,
Lost in dreams that light the way.

The silver glow, a gentle touch,
In slumber's hold, we crave so much.
Celestial paths unfold above,
While hearts entwine in endless love.

A tapestry of hope and care,
In starlit dreams, we're free to dare.
To wander realms where wishes soar,
In cosmic arms, forevermore.

As dawn breaks forth, we find our place,
Awakening from night's embrace.
Yet in our souls, the dream remains,
In the starlit skies, love's sweet refrains.

The Drift of Hopeful Horizons

Across the sea, where dreams unfold,
Horizons beckon, bright and bold.
With every wave, our spirits rise,
In the drift, we touch the skies.

The sunlit path, it calls our name,
Through distant lands, a yearning flame.
With every step, the fears subside,
In heart's embrace, we boldly stride.

With every breath, the world expands,
Together, we weave our plans.
The journey's long, yet moments gleam,
In every drift, we chase the dream.

As evening falls, the stars ignite,
Guiding us through the tranquil night.
With hopeful hearts, we chart the course,
In life's great drift, we find our source.

A Tapestry of Gentle Rest

In twilight's glow, the day departs,
With whispered winds, it calms our hearts.
A tapestry of peace unfurls,
In gentle rest, our spirit twirls.

Soft shadows dance upon the floor,
Embracing us, we yearn for more.
With every sigh, the world slows down,
As evening wraps its velvet gown.

Hushed are the sounds, the chaos fades,
In quietude, our joy cascades.
The moonbeams weave a lullaby,
While stars above begin to sigh.

In dreams, we drift on silver streams,
A canvas filled with endless dreams.
In gentle rest, we find our home,
A tapestry where hearts can roam.

The Slumbering Sky's Serenade

A blanket of stars softly glows,
Whispers of night in the breeze flows,
Dreams drift gently on lunar beams,
Wrapped in the silence of moonlit dreams.

Clouds like pillows float high above,
Cradling the night with a tender love,
The cosmos hums a lullaby sweet,
As night treads softly with silent feet.

Winds carry tales of the dusk's embrace,
Painting the sky with delicate grace,
Each twinkle a story, each fade a spark,
In the heart of the vast and timeless dark.

As slumbering skies take their repose,
In their quiet beauty, our spirit grows,
We find our peace in twilight's sigh,
Beneath the serenade of the slumbering sky.

Sails of Fog on Dream's Voyage

Soft whispers of mist weave tales anew,
Sailing the seas where dreams drift through,
Waves of wonder caress the shore,
Guiding lost hearts to a hidden door.

Sails of starlight, shimmering white,
Glide through the shadows of the night,
Each ripple a memory, each gust a grace,
Finding our journey in time and space.

The horizon dances with hopes aglow,
Carried away where the wild winds blow,
Through realms of magic, we're gently cast,
In the sacred waters of dreams vast.

With each heartbeat, the world unfurls,
Embracing the mystery of life's swirls,
On sails of fog, we traverse the skies,
Awakening wonder before our eyes.

The Tranquil Veil of Nocturne

In the arms of night, solace is found,
Wrapped in a silence, so deep and profound,
Stars sprinkle light like whispers of dreams,
Bathing the world in their glimmering beams.

The gentle moon rises, a guardian bright,
Casting a glow on the canvas of night,
With every heartbeat, the stillness draws near,
In the tranquil embrace, we hold our fear.

Soft breezes carry the scents of the dark,
Perfumed with echoes of nature's spark,
In the lull of the night, our spirits take flight,
Beneath the vast heavens, our souls ignite.

Nocturne's veil wraps us in its care,
As we drift on dreams to otherwhere,
In this peaceful realm where all is well,
In the tranquil veil, our hearts shall dwell.

A Resting Place in the Firmament

High above the world, in a twilight space,
Clouds pause to witness the stars' embrace,
Each glowing dot, a wish held tight,
In this resting place, the heart feels light.

With every flicker, a story is spun,
Of hopes and dreams that have just begun,
In the firmament, we find our way,
Guided by starlight that never fades.

The universe whispers with ancient grace,
Inviting us in, to find our place,
In the cradle of night, we gently sway,
Finding solace in the dawn's soft display.

A resting place, where all can be free,
To dance in the ether, to simply be,
In the firmament's arms, we'll always belong,
Under celestial tunes, we hum our song.

The Purr of Midnight's Breath

Whispers soar in twilight's keep,
The shadows dance, the secrets seep.
Beneath the moon, a gentle sigh,
The night unfolds, the stars comply.

Fingers trace the velvet air,
A melody, light as a prayer.
In silence, dreams begin to weave,
A tapestry of hopes we believe.

Each heartbeat echoes in the dark,
Awakening the silent spark.
With every breath, the world anew,
The purr of night, a soothing cue.

Softly now, let worries fade,
In midnight's arms, serenely laid.
The purr of life, a tender guide,
As dawn approaches, dreams abide.

The Enchanted Lull in the Cosmos

Stars shimmer like tender eyes,
In the vastness, a lullaby flies.
Galaxies swirl with whispered grace,
Embracing all in this timeless space.

The moon spills silver on the sea,
Rippling with cosmic reverie.
Planets glide in a tranquil dance,
Each moment a fleeting chance.

Cradled by the weightless air,
Heartbeats synchronize with care.
Infinite tales in starlight spun,
A lull that cradles everyone.

In the cosmic arms, we gently sway,
Lost in night's enchanting play.
The lull a spell, a gentle thread,
We drift through dreams, through time we tread.

The Still Air Wearing Dreams

Upon the edge of twilight's breath,
The stillness wraps the earth in guise.
Each moment held, a promise kept,
While dreams weave softly in the skies.

The breeze, a whisper from afar,
Inviting hope to dance and twirl.
In starlit swirls, we dare to dream,
In stillness, beauty starts to unfurl.

With every sigh, the night invokes,
A realm where hearts and wishes meet.
The air, a canvas, softly strokes,
Each heartbeat paints a tale so sweet.

And as the world begins to fade,
We find our dreams in silence draped.
The still air wears the night's embrace,
A haven where our souls find space.

Soothe Me under Starlit Skies

Beneath the vaulted, endless blue,
A gentle breeze begins to sigh.
Stars twinkle like a lover's cue,
Soothe me now, beneath the sky.

The night opens its tender hands,
To cradle worries in the dark.
In whispered notes, a tune expands,
As dreams ignite, a hopeful spark.

Let moonlight paint the world in gold,
With every glow, my heart takes flight.
In this embrace, I find the bold,
A cosmic comfort in the night.

So hold me close till morning breaks,
In softened light, our spirits rise.
Beneath the stars, my heart awakes,
Soothe me, love, under starlit skies.

Fleeting Visions in the Ether

Dreams drift softly like clouds,
Whispers of colors unseen.
In the stillness they linger,
Glimmers of what might have been.

Across the fabric of time,
Threads of silver entwine.
Moments fleeting like shadows,
Echoes of lives so divine.

The dance of stars fades slowly,
Into the arms of the night.
Each thought a flickering flame,
Brief sparks of distant light.

As visions dissolve in the mist,
Leaving traces on the skin.
We chase what is merely a wisp,
The beauty of where we've been.

A Somnolent Sojourn

Softly the moon drapes her veil,
Crickets serenade the air.
The world in gentle repose,
As dreams weave tales everywhere.

Wander through fields of silken calm,
Where shadows play where they will.
Each sigh a feathered whisper,
Floating on winds, sweet and still.

Time slows, a fountain of rest,
As starlight kisses the ground.
In the arms of slumber we rest,
Healing where hope can be found.

Awake in the warmth of dawn,
With echoes of night softly fade.
A somnolent journey we take,
In solace, our hearts are laid.

Beneath the Blanket of Night

Veils of darkness spread wide,
Cradling dreams in their fold.
Secrets whispered through shadows,
In the quiet, tales unfold.

Stars like diamonds are scattered,
Glimmers on a canvas deep.
Within this silent expanse,
Our hopes and hearts gently sleep.

The whispers of wind weave sweet,
An embrace that feels divine.
Midnight's calm wraps around me,
A moment, pure and benign.

Beneath the blanket of night,
I find solace, find my way.
In the company of silence,
A promise of a new day.

Silent Lull of the Universe

In the quiet of the cosmos,
Stars hum a soothing tune.
Galaxies drift and shimmer,
Cradled in the embrace of the moon.

Each heartbeat of stardust glows,
A lullaby that transcends.
Whispers of worlds yet to be,
As time bends and smoothly bends.

The universe breathes softly,
With tranquility in its core.
In this silent symphony,
I find myself wanting more.

A dance of light and shadow,
In every twinkle, a story told.
The lull of the cosmos surrounds,
A magic waiting to unfold.

Whispers of the Dreamscape

In twilight's hush, the shadows play,
Soft echoes of the night display.
A world where silence breathes and sighs,
Beneath the vast and starry skies.

Threads of silver weave the light,
Guiding dreams through endless night.
Each whisper holds a fleeting chance,
To lift the soul in gentle dance.

Through valleys deep and mountains high,
The secrets dance, the spirits fly.
In every heartbeat, mysteries bloom,
Awakening the silent gloom.

So close your eyes, embrace the sound,
Where dreams and reality are found.
In whispers soft, the heart will roam,
In the dreamscape, we find our home.

Lullabies in the Sky

Softly the stars begin to gleam,
Cradling thoughts in a gentle dream.
Moonlight weaves through clouds of gray,
Lullabies drift, calming the fray.

Each note a caress in the night,
Guiding lost souls towards the light.
With every sigh, a wish takes flight,
Painting hopes in the quiet twilight.

In the embrace of soothing air,
Whispers of love linger everywhere.
Stars align with tales of old,
In lullabies, our hearts are told.

So close your eyes, let worries cease,
With lullabies, we find our peace.
In the expanse where dreams resound,
A world of magic will be found.

The Celestial Cradle

In the arms of night, softly curled,
The cosmos sings to a wandering world.
Stars like mothers in gentle sway,
Guide lost spirits who long to stay.

Each twinkle, a kiss from above,
A promise wrapped in endless love.
Cradled within the velvet sea,
Whispers of fate set our hearts free.

Galaxies spin in a graceful dance,
Offering hope in every glance.
Beyond the limits of time and space,
In the cradle of night, we find our place.

So drift away on wings of light,
As dreams take form in the fading night.
In the celestial embrace we soar,
Forever held, forever more.

Veils of Midnight Drift

Beneath the cloak of shadows deep,
Where secrets hide and echoes sleep.
The midnight air, like whispers soft,
Carries tales of dreams aloft.

Veils of mist wrap the world tight,
Hiding wonders from our sight.
Each breath we take, a silent wish,
Floating in the stillness, a gentle kiss.

Stars peer through the silken thread,
Guiding the lost, where hope is fed.
In the quiet gloom, our hearts intertwine,
Beneath the veils, the light will shine.

So wander deep through the velvet night,
Where veils of magic veil the light.
Embrace the shadows, let spirits drift,
Together we dance, a timeless gift.

A Realm Where Time Is Still

In shadows deep, the whispers play,
A world where moments melt away.
The sun hangs low, the moon stands high,
As time drifts past with a gentle sigh.

Waves of silence, softly flow,
Carrying dreams we do not know.
Each heartbeat lingers, soft and bright,
In this realm wrapped warm, in the night.

The trees hold secrets, ancient and wise,
Their leaves dance slow beneath the skies.
In stillness found, our souls unfurl,
Lost in the magic of this twirling world.

Here time breathes slow, a tender friend,
Where every story has no end.
In a quiet embrace, we gently stand,
In a timeless stretch of golden sand.

The Drifting Pages of Night

Stars emerge from twilight's cloak,
Each shimmered light a tale bespoke.
The moon writes verses on the deep,
In the silence, secrets seep.

Whispers linger on the breeze,
Carrying wishes, soft and free.
Pages turning in the dark,
Each flicker holding its own spark.

Dreams entwine in a tapestry,
Woven from night's sweet mystery.
Silent stories, hearts ignite,
In the drifting pages of night.

Eclipsed by shadows, thoughts take flight,
Carried softly by the night.
In each moment, a chance to roam,
Within the pages, we find home.

Veil of the Resting Stars

A veil of stars, a tender glow,
Cradles dreams in hushed flow.
Softly scattered, they shine above,
Guiding hearts with endless love.

The night enfolds all in its grace,
Each twinkle holds a hidden place.
Amongst the vast, a soul reveals,
The truths that silence gently heals.

Underneath this starry shroud,
Whispers form a gentle cloud.
While shadows dance on silver streams,
The veil protects our deepest dreams.

A sanctuary in the dark,
Where light ignites a hopeful spark.
In the quiet, stars will guide,
Veils of magic, side by side.

Lull of the Enchanted Winds

The winds are singing through the trees,
A lullaby that sways with ease.
Each note a story, soft and light,
Cradling the earth in a gentle night.

Whispers brush against the skin,
Carried tales from where we've been.
In every breeze, a secret stirs,
Through fields and valleys, softly purrs.

Enchantments weave in twilight's breath,
Embraced by calm, a dance with death.
Where shadows linger, dreams ignite,
In lull of winds, we find our flight.

With every sigh, the heart aligns,
To the rhythm of life's sweet designs.
And as the night wraps us in trust,
We float on winds of wanderlust.

The Sweet Arcana of Dreaming

In shadows soft, the visions stir,
A tapestry where hope may blur.
With each new dawn, they drift away,
Yet in the heart, their echoes stay.

Beneath the stars, our thoughts take flight,
Whispers of love in the velvet night.
Each cherished dream, a fleeting song,
We chase the light, where we belong.

In silent realms, the soul will roam,
Through radiant skies, we find our home.
With every sigh, the secrets greet,
The sweet arcana in slumber's heat.

As dawn unveils the mystic's art,
The dreams we hold, forever part.
In waking hours, their traces gleam,
The magic found in every dream.

The Opal Calm of Dusk

The opal sky in twilight's grace,
Reflects the peace in every face.
The world grows dim, the stars awake,
In whispered tones, the shadows break.

As day gives way to gentle night,
The horizon melts, a painter's sight.
Silence wraps the evening's glow,
In calming hues, our worries slow.

With every breeze, the secrets sway,
In twilight's hush, we gently lay.
The night unfolds like a velvet thread,
In dreams untold, where hearts are led.

Beneath the arch of fading light,
The opal calm brings sweet delight.
In this embrace, we find our peace,
A tranquil pause that will not cease.

Coasting on a Whispering Breeze

Upon the waves of a dreamt-up sea,
I find the whispers speak to me.
The gentle wind, a lover's sigh,
In twilight's arms, we learn to fly.

Each rustling leaf holds tales of old,
In windswept paths where secrets unfold.
With every gust, the world transforms,
In soothing tones, the heart conforms.

The breeze that sways the branches high,
Carries our hopes to the open sky.
We glide along with ease and grace,
In nature's tune, we find our place.

Coasting softly on life's sweet air,
The journey flows, beyond compare.
In every breath, a story we weave,
On whispering winds, we dare believe.

Dreams Nurtured in Twilight's Hue

In twilight's glow, where wishes bloom,
We plant our hopes in evening's room.
The stars ignite, a canvas bright,
With dreams nurtured in soft moonlight.

Each fleeting thought, like petals fall,
In gentle darkness, we heed their call.
With every glance, new visions spark,
As shadows stretch and light grows dark.

In this embrace, the world slows down,
As night unveils its jeweled crown.
The heartbeats dance, a tender beat,
Where dreams and twilight softly meet.

Through whispered nights and velvet skies,
Our aspirations learn to rise.
In every hue, a promise lives,
In dreams nurtured, the spirit gives.

A Tapestry of Dreamed Reflections

In the weft of twilight's glow,
Threads of silver softly flow,
Whispers carried by the night,
Painting shadows, chasing light.

Memories entwined in streams,
Woven tightly, stitched in dreams,
Each a tale of love and loss,
Fleeting moments, paths we cross.

Tangles of desire and fear,
Echoes of the heart so clear,
We explore this fabric vast,
Search for peace amid the past.

Yet in this quilt, warmth resides,
Mapping journeys, hopes, and tides,
With each thread, a story spun,
A tapestry, our lives as one.

Beneath the Gossamer Dawn

Awakening in soft embrace,
Morning whispers, a gentle grace,
Stars retreat with velvet sighs,
As the sun begins to rise.

Golden rays kiss the dew,
Nature wakes with colors new,
Each petal unfurls with light,
Painting dreams in pure delight.

Birdsongs weave a bright refrain,
Through the stillness, joy will reign,
Life unfolds in vibrant hues,
As the world breathes in the views.

Beneath the arcs of pale blue skies,
Hope awakens, softly flies,
In the dawn, we find our way,
A new beginning, every day.

The Quiet Lull of the Universe

In the vastness, silence hums,
Stars like distant, muted drums,
Galaxies in a gentle swirl,
Whispers of a cosmic pearl.

Time slows down in the twilight,
Galactic dreams take wing in flight,
Comets trail with fleeting grace,
In this void, we find our place.

Nebulae breathe in colors rare,
Woven lights in endless air,
Each heartbeat echoes through the dark,
Nature's lull, a glowing spark.

Wrapped in the universe's quilt,
Every starlit path is built,
In silence, we connect anew,
A quiet lull, the cosmos' view.

Night's Soft Womb of Rest

Beneath the moon's gentle gaze,
The world dissolves in twilight haze,
Wrapped in dreams, the heart takes flight,
In night's embrace, all feels right.

Softly whispers lull the mind,
Where worries fade and peace we find,
In shadows deep, serenity flows,
As the quiet night softly grows.

Stars are scattered, twinkling bright,
Guiding souls through soothing night,
Each breath a step toward the dawn,
In this cocoon, we are reborn.

Drift away on silken clouds,
Lost in warmth, obscured by shrouds,
Night cradles us, a tender host,
In its womb, we find our post.

Shadows Wrapped in Moonlight

In the stillness of the night,
Shadows dance with soft delight.
Whispers weave through silver trees,
Carried gently by the breeze.

Stars above begin to sing,
Melodies the night does bring.
Every shadow finds its place,
Wrapped in moonlight's warm embrace.

Lanterns of the darkened sky,
Guide the spirits drifting by.
In the quiet, dreams take flight,
Underneath the watchful light.

Moments linger, time stands still,
Hearts entwined with nature's will.
In this realm, the world feels bright,
In shadows wrapped, the heart takes flight.

Beneath the Gentle Abyss

Beneath the surface, silence sighs,
Hidden depths and starry skies.
Secrets float on waves of night,
Cradled in the soft moonlight.

Whispers call from ocean floors,
Tales of magic, ancient shores.
With each ripple, spirits dance,
In the dark, a fleeting chance.

Breath of tides, a lullaby,
Sings of dreams that drift and fly.
In the depths, where shadows play,
Life and mystery find their way.

Awakened by the midnight tide,
Where the fears and hopes collide.
Beneath the calm, the world does stir,
In the gentle abyss, we confer.

Ethereal Hues of Rest

Softly painted skies of dusk,
Whisper secrets, sweet and husk.
Colors blend in twilight's kiss,
A moment's peace, a precious bliss.

Lavender and amber glide,
Cradled close, the stars reside.
In this hour, worries cease,
Wrapped in hues of gentle peace.

Feathery clouds in shadows drift,
Nature's night-time, tender gift.
As the world sighs deep and long,
Ethereal hues invite the song.

Rest is found in soft embrace,
Time slows down, a slower pace.
In these colors, hearts can mend,
To the quiet, we descend.

Night's Embrace

In night's embrace, the silence grows,
Cascading dreams, where memory flows.
Beneath the stars, all fears relent,
In the dark, our souls are lent.

The moonlight bathes the earth in glow,
Filling spaces where shadows flow.
Whispers linger in the air,
Moments of peace beyond compare.

Every heartbeat echoes soft,
Carried high, as dreams take off.
In this realm, where time unwinds,
Night's embrace, the heart finds.

Wrapped in velvet, soft and deep,
Cradled gently, drift to sleep.
In the still, where worlds entwine,
Night's embrace, a love divine.

Sleep's Silken Embrace

Softly drifting on night's tide,
Whispers of the stars abide.
Moonlit beams weave through the dark,
Cradling dreams with tender spark.

Gentle lullabies take flight,
Kissing troubles out of sight.
Wrapped in warmth, the world unwinds,
In this haven, peace we find.

Each heartbeat slows, serene delight,
As shadows dance in pale moonlight.
Sleep's embrace, a silken thread,
Weaving visions in the head.

Tomorrow waits beyond the dawn,
But for now, we gently yawn.
In dreamy realms, we'll softly roam,
Till waking brings us safely home.

Shadows of a Drowsy Sky

Whispers float on twilight's sigh,
As drowsy clouds drift on high.
Beneath the veil of night so deep,
The world around begins to sleep.

Stars peek out, a scattered guide,
As moonlight dances, soft and wide.
In this hush, our worries cease,
Finding solace, finding peace.

Every shadow finds its place,
Gentle night, a warm embrace.
Through the whispers, dreams unfold,
In their arms, brave hearts grow bold.

Silhouettes in quiet grace,
In the stillness, find your space.
Let the night wrap you up tight,
Cradled in the soft moonlight.

Dreams Born from Eiderdowns

Nestled close in pillowed bliss,
Whispers float in gentle mist.
Eiderdowns, so soft, so light,
Cradle dreams in velvet night.

Every thought drifts like a plume,
As the stars begin to bloom.
In this world of night's embrace,
Time slows down, we find our pace.

Fleeting visions softly sway,
Carried forth by night's ballet.
Each sigh dances in the air,
Spinning hopes, casting care.

In warmth we find a sacred ground,
Where sleepy hearts are gently bound.
Dreams are born, as shadows flow,
In soft layers, let life glow.

The Hush of Starlit Rest

Underneath a starlit dome,
Whispers beckon, drawing home.
In the hush, the world feels small,
Wrapped in night's enchanted thrall.

Gentle breezes brush my face,
Bringing calm, a warm embrace.
In this quiet, fears release,
Finding comfort, finding peace.

Softly tucked 'neath cosmic light,
Drifting softly into night.
Every heartbeat slows and sighs,
As the universe replies.

As sleep falls like velvet rain,
In the stillness, free from pain.
In this moment, let it be,
The starlit rest will set you free.

Mists of Quietude

In the calm embrace of dawn,
Whispers weave through the air,
Veils of silence upon the lawn,
Nature holds its breath with care.

Gentle streams hum a soft tune,
Leaves dance lightly on the breeze,
Underneath the silver moon,
Stillness wrapped in twilight's tease.

Fog blankets the sleeping reeds,
Stars blink softly from afar,
Crickets play where silence leads,
Mists twinkle like a distant star.

A world held close in shadows deep,
Quietude spreading far and wide,
In this moment, silence steep,
Nature's beauty, our hearts abide.

Nights Swaddled in Stillness

Stars blink softly overhead,
Moonlight bathes the world in glow,
The night whispers, secrets spread,
A lullaby, so sweet and slow.

Trees stand guard, serene and tall,
Their branches cradle dreams anew,
In the silence, soft and small,
Time extends, the moments brew.

Each breath taken, a gentle sigh,
The earth unfolds her hidden grace,
Night enfolds us, draws us nigh,
In stillness, we find our place.

Wrapped in shadows, peace takes flight,
Every heartbeat, a calming sound,
Nights swaddled in the velvet light,
In this hush, true solace found.

A Dance of Drowsy Shadows

In twilight's grasp, shadows sway,
A gentle waltz upon the ground,
Softly drifting, they play,
In the night, their grace unbound.

Silhouettes twirl with whispered sighs,
Embracing dreams where moments blend,
With every move, the quiet flies,
Drowsy hearts find ways to mend.

Night unfurls its velvet cloak,
Caressing thoughts that drift away,
In this stillness, silence spoke,
As shadows dance at end of day.

Under stars that softly gleam,
A ballet played on moonlight's stage,
In the hush, we drift and dream,
As drowsy shadows turn the page.

Feathers of Forgotten Dreams

Whispers float on the evening air,
Carried soft by a breath of night,
Feathers drift without a care,
Remnants of dreams lost from sight.

Beneath the surface, echoes sleep,
In the stillness, they softly sigh,
Into the silence, secrets creep,
Wrapped in memories, they fly.

Glimmers of hope, once brightly shone,
Now cradled in the heart's deep seam,
Gentle reminders, never gone,
Feathers float on the edge of dream.

Each moment holds its whispered tale,
Of what was, and what's yet to be,
In shadows where soft memories sail,
Feathers guide us, wild and free.

Floating on a Lullaby

A whisper flows on gentle air,
Soft notes that dance without a care.
They cradle dreams in tender light,
And guide the heart through starry night.

With every breath, the melody sways,
As shadows play in twilight's gaze.
A symphony of peace unfolds,
In lullabies, the soul beholds.

The moonlight weaves a silver thread,
Through quiet realms where spirits tread.
In blissful harmony we drift,
On this sweet song, our spirits lift.

In dreams we float, so far away,
Where worries fade and hearts can stay.
Each note a balm, each rest a sigh,
Forever bound, just you and I.

The Gentle Drift of Twilight

Twilight whispers soft and slow,
As colors blend in evening's glow.
The sun dips low, the skies ignite,
In hues of lavender and light.

A tranquil hush envelops all,
As shadows stretch and nightbirds call.
The world transforms in dusky tones,
A peaceful canvas, nature's moans.

With every breath, the stars align,
In this serenity divine.
The gentle drift of night's embrace,
Invites the heart to find its space.

In this soft veil, we find our way,
Through fleeting thoughts and twilight play.
A moment held, forever dear,
In the drift of twilight's sphere.

Veils of Serene Silence

Beneath the stars, a silence weaves,
In shadows deep, my heart believes.
The world dissolves in quiet peace,
And all the worries start to cease.

A gentle sway of moonlit air,
Embracing dreams without a care.
In veils of night, we wander free,
Lost in the echoes of the sea.

With every breath, serenity blooms,
As whispers dance in soft-gloomed rooms.
In silence, spirits intertwine,
Creating worlds where hearts align.

The night unfurls its tender grace,
In every shadow, find your place.
In veils of calm, our souls shall glide,
Together, here, we shall abide.

In the Arms of Midnight

In the arms of midnight, dreams take flight,
Draped in darkness, soft as night.
Each breath a whisper, sweet and low,
As silver stars begin to glow.

Time stands still in this sacred space,
Where shadows linger, soft embrace.
Gentle lullabies weave through the air,
As hopes and sorrows blend with care.

In quiet moments, hearts align,
As moonlit paths begin to shine.
The world outside fades far away,
In midnight's arms, we long to stay.

With every heartbeat, secrets flow,
Beneath the stars, our spirits grow.
In the stillness, love's light ignites,
Forever cradled in the nights.

Floating on Starry Pillows

Upon the clouds, we drift and sway,
Beneath the night, in soft array.
Each twinkle sings, a lullaby,
As dreams take flight, we softly sigh.

The moonlight bathes our gentle dreams,
In silver hues, the starlight beams.
We ride the waves of whispered air,
In cosmic dance, without a care.

Embraced by night, we find our peace,
In floating realms, our hearts release.
Where fantasies and wishes blend,
On starry pillows, we transcend.

A journey forged in night's embrace,
With every star, we find our place.
Together on this heavenly ride,
In boundless skies, we will abide.

The Softness of Hibernation

In quiet woods, the world retreats,
Blankets of snow, where silence greets.
Nature breathes in a gentle sigh,
As winter whispers, soft and shy.

The trees stand still, adorned in white,
While dreams cocoon in the soft night.
Creatures burrow, snug and warm,
In hidden nests, away from harm.

The stillness wraps in tender care,
A peaceful pause in frosty air.
Lulled by the calm, we rest our heads,
In nature's arms, where magic spreads.

Awaiting spring, we close our eyes,
In dreams of blooms and starry skies.
For in this hush, we find our way,
In softness, we shall gently stay.

Fantasies in a Twilight Veil

As dusk descends with colors bright,
The world transforms in soft twilight.
Shadows dance upon the ground,
In whispers, secrets can be found.

The horizon blurs in hues so deep,
Where echoes linger, and shadows creep.
In this ethereal, patient glow,
Fantasies awaken, soft and slow.

Stars begin to twinkle high,
Painting dreams across the sky.
In twilight's calm, let visions spin,
As day retreats and night begins.

With every breath, the magic grows,
In twilight's arms, the mystery flows.
Lost in dreams, we roam and sail,
Embraced in love's twilight veil.

Serenity Amongst the Stars

In quiet nights, the heavens gleam,
Whispers of starlight softly beam.
Among the celestial spheres we find,
A gentle touch that calms the mind.

The constellations softly glow,
As cosmic winds begin to flow.
With every twinkle, peace is sown,
In this vast world, we are not alone.

The silence wraps around our souls,
In starry depths, our spirit trolls.
We seek the warmth of distant lights,
In tranquil dreams, on endless nights.

Together here, we'll always share,
The serenity that fills the air.
Amongst the stars, our hearts take flight,
In eternal love, we find our light.

Woven Threads of Midnight Dreams

In twilight's cloak, sweet visions weave,
A tapestry of hopes we believe.
Stars whisper tales of yearn and grace,
In slumber's arms, we find our place.

Moonlight dances on dreams' gentle streams,
Casting shadows on our silent schemes.
Woven threads, both fragile and bold,
In the night's embrace, our hearts unfold.

Chasing echoes through realms of night,
Where wishes soar and shadows take flight.
With every breath, the magic stirs,
In woven dreams, the soul endures.

Awake we shall, with dawn's soft light,
But memories linger, sweet and bright.
In every thread, a story's spun,
Woven dreams unite, never done.

Slumber's Secret Garden

Beneath the stars, in dreams we roam,
A secret garden, far from home.
Whispers of flowers, sweetly bloom,
In twilight's hush, dispelling gloom.

Moonlit petals caress the night,
Softly glowing, a gentle sight.
In this haven, worries fade,
As dreams unfurl in soft cascade.

Each moment tender, time stands still,
Nature's chorus, a serenade thrill.
In slumber's arms, we find our peace,
A garden where all sorrows cease.

Awake we shall, yet carry near,
The fragrance of dreams that persevere.
In our hearts, that garden stays,
A sanctuary of love's warm rays.

Embrace of the Soft Winds

Through whispering trees, the soft winds play,
Carrying secrets of night and day.
They dance with shadows, swirling around,
In their embrace, true solace found.

Gentle breezes brush against our skin,
Stirring memories deep from within.
They sing of journeys, long and wide,
In the wind's arms, we safely glide.

A symphony of nature's sighs,
Painting the world 'neath open skies.
With every gust, the heart takes flight,
In soft winds' embrace, we feel delight.

As dawn approaches, the winds retreat,
Yet their sweet whispers remain discreet.
In every breath, their love remains,
In life's embrace, where peace refrains.

The Whispering Veil of Solitude

In quiet corners, shadows gleam,
The whispering veil, a tranquil dream.
Wrapped in silence, thoughts take flight,
In solitude's arms, we find the light.

Like autumn leaves, drifting slow,
The heart uncovers what we don't show.
Each gentle sigh, a secret shared,
The veil of peace, deeply cared.

Time stands still in the hush we crave,
A sacred space, our spirits save.
In solitude's embrace, we redefine,
The strength in silence, truly divine.

As moments pass, clarity grows,
In the whispering veil, the heart knows.
With every breath, we build anew,
In solitude's grace, we find what's true.

The Gently Resting Heavens

In twilight's hush, the stars align,
Soft whispers drift, a gentle sign.
The moon hangs low, a silver thread,
As dreams awaken, softly spread.

The clouds like pillows, float on high,
With secret thoughts the night does sigh.
A canvas deep of velvet blue,
Where hopes and wishes shimmer through.

Beneath the gaze of watchful skies,
The world rests quiet, softly lies.
In calm embrace, hearts find their way,
To dance with night, till break of day.

As dawn approaches, fades the glow,
Yet in our hearts, the night will flow.
The gently resting heavens stay,
To guide our dreams through light of day.

Shimmering Haze of Peace

In morning mist, the world awakes,
A shimmering dance that gently shakes.
The golden rays break through the gray,
As nature sings a sweet ballet.

Soft breezes carry whispers clear,
Of tranquil thoughts that draw us near.
A haze of peace enwraps the land,
Embracing all with tender hand.

With every bloom, a story grows,
In colors bright, the beauty glows.
Each step we take on dew-kissed grass,
A journey shared, let moments pass.

As day unfolds, the heart aligns,
In shimmering hues, our spirit finds.
A gentle hush, a calming space,
In the embrace of peace's grace.

Resplendent Dreams Adrift

In twilight's realm, where shadows play,
Resplendent dreams begin to sway.
Soft melodies float on the breeze,
Encircled by the whispering trees.

Like wisps of fog, they intertwine,
In visions bright, the stars align.
With every heartbeat, soaring high,
To dance with hopes that touch the sky.

Through realms of light, our thoughts will soar,
As echoes of the past explore.
A tapestry of what could be,
Awakening our spirits free.

In slumber's grasp, we drift away,
On waves of dreams, from night to day.
Resplendent visions fade from view,
Yet linger on, in hearts so true.

A Voyage through Velvet Night

Beneath the cloak of velvet night,
We set our sails, our hearts in flight.
With stars as guides, the moon's soft glow,
We journey forth, where dreams can grow.

The softest waves, a lullaby,
As whispers of the night drift by.
In every corner, secrets stir,
As shadows dance and visions blur.

A canvas dark, alive with lore,
In tides of time, we search for more.
With every heartbeat, we explore,
The deep unknown, a silent shore.

For in the night, our souls ignite,
A voyage bold 'neath stars so bright.
Embracing all, both fear and light,
We sail forever through the night.